Faith vs. Fear

Faith vs. Fear

It Is Your Choice

Brenda Williams

Kingdom Living Publishing
Accokeek, MD 20607

Author's photographs by Magic Glamour
www.magicglamour.com

Published by

Kingdom Living Publishing
P.O. Box 660
Accokeek, MD 20607

ISBN 978-0-9968089-6-5

Printed in the United States of America.
For worldwide distribution.

Content

Introduction

Faith vs. Fear is something that we all face every day. There are all types of fear, some greater than others. However, God has given to every believer a measure of faith. In the Scriptures, we read about little faith, great faith, mountain-moving faith. Sometimes we wonder how our faith will grow from one level to another level. What do I need to do to increase my faith? Should I pray for more faith? How can I move from fear to faith? These are all thoughts that I am sure have crossed your mind during your journey to walk with the Father.

This book will help you understand what faith is and what to do when fear tries to overtake you. Study the following Scriptures about faith and fear:

Hebrews 11:1

*Now **faith is** the substance of things hoped for, the evidence of things not seen.*

Romans 12:3

For I say, through the grace given to me, to everyone who is among you, not to think of himself more highly than he ought to think, but to think soberly, as God has dealt to each one a measure of faith.

Romans 1:16

*For I am not ashamed of the gospel of Christ, for it is the power of God **to** salvation for everyone who **believes**, for the Jew first and also for the Greek.*

Galatians 3:22

*But the Scripture has confined all under sin, that the promise by **faith** in Jesus Christ might be given **to** those who **believe**.*

Hebrews 11:6

*But without **faith** it is impossible **to** please Him, for he who comes **to** God must **believe** that He is,* *and that He is a rewarder of those who diligently seek Him.*

2 Timothy 1:7

*For **God has not given us a spirit of fear**, but **of** power **and of** love **and of a** sound mind.*

1 John 4:18

*There is no **fear** in love; but perfect love casts out **fear**, because **fear** involves **torment**. But he who **fears has** not been made perfect in love.*

Faith is believing the Word of God is true and acting on what the Word says to do. Faith is trusting God to lead and guide us every day and not trying to do things in our own strength. We have to acknowledge Him in everything that we do.

Proverbs 3:5-6

Trust in the LORD with all your heart, And lean not on your own understanding; in all your ways acknowledge Him, And He shall direct your paths.

The fear of the Lord is the beginning of wisdom. There are some good fears, e.g., reverential fear of God is good. That is the type of fear we all should have.

Psalm 111:10

The fear of the Lord is the beginning of wisdom; *A good understanding have all those who do His commandments. His praise endures forever.*

Proverbs 1:7

The fear of the Lord is the beginning of *knowledge, But fools despise* ***wisdom*** *and instruction.*

Proverbs 9:10

*"**The fear of the Lord is the beginning of wisdom,** And **the** knowledge **of the** Holy One **is** understanding.*

The fear that I am sharing in this book is the type of fear that hinders you from moving in the things of God, the kind that brings torment.

I have personally experienced all types of fear in my life. As I began to study the Word of God and meditate in the Word, I know that the faith that God has given to me is growing every day. Sometimes we can have great faith in one area of our lives, and in another area, our faith can be weak.

I have learned to trust God in everything, because I cannot do anything without Him. He is my constant companion, my friend, my confidant, my healer, my provider. I have learned that everything I stand in need of He will and does provide.

When I mess up, I am quick to repent and ask for forgiveness, and He forgives and restores. He is a great God, and there is nothing impossible for Him. When we pray and ask for things that do not come when we want, we must wait on His timing. He knows our end from our beginning. His ways are so much higher than our little finite thinking. It all comes down to trust.

Do we trust God to do what His Word says? Do we believe Him? There are no expiration dates on our prayers. I learned this by reading Mark Batterson's book *"The Circle Maker."* When I think about that, I know the prayers that my grandmother prayed for me are coming to pass now. So, I continue to stand in faith and wait on God's timing.

Notes and Reflections

Expectations

We must expect God to honor his Word. He has watched and continues to watch over His Word to perform it in our lives. Jesus is the living Word. Jesus and the Word are the same. In John 1:1, we see, *"In the beginning was the Word, and the Word was with God, and the Word was God."* John 1:14 says, *"And the Word was made flesh and dwelt among us...."*

All the promises in the Bible are for the children of God. If we have accepted Him as our savior, those promises are for us. He has given us faith to believe Him, and if we believe Him, we can expect Him to do what His Word says. We ask, believe, and expect the answer.

As parents, we expect our children to obey us when we tell them what to do. We expect to get paid when we go to work and do our jobs. We know on pay day we will get a check for the time that we worked. So, why is it that we do not expect God to answer our prayers when we pray according to the Word? When we do not receive the answer, during the time we think appropriate, we question whether God heard our prayer or denied it. We need to remember that our timing is not His timing. His ways are so much higher than our ways.

Sometimes, we need to check ourselves out first before we pray. Ask yourself these questions:

1. Is there any unforgiveness in my heart?
2. What are the motives behind this request?
3. How do I treat co-workers, neighbors, or family?
4. Have I done the last thing the Holy Spirit asked me to do?
5. Do I offer praise and thanksgiving to God for the things He has already done for me?
6. How is my prayer life?
7. Do I only pray when I want something?
8. Do I really want to hear the answer, or do I want to do what I want to do?

If we can honestly answer these questions before we pray, we can expect to hear an answer to our prayers.

Abraham believed God, and it was accounted to him as righteousness. In Genesis 22, God told Abraham to sacrifice his son Isaac, and he was prepared to do it. When Abraham and his son journeyed to the mountain to offer a burnt offering, Isaac asked about the lamb for the burnt offering since it was not among their belongings. Abraham responded, "The Lord will provide," and they went on their way. God did provide. I believe that Abraham was prepared to offer Isaac as an offering. He knew if he did offer his son that God would provide another son. He trusted God. He knew that God had told him that he would have many sons and daughters.

Joseph was a dreamer, and he told his brothers about his dreams. However, they did not like Joseph because his dreams always had him in a place of authority over them. Joseph had expectations that his dreams would come to pass, and they did. But Joseph went through a lot before the dreams finally manifested. He believed God and trusted in Him, and through all the circumstances, he remained faithful to the things of God (Genesis Chapters 37-41).

We must believe God and that the promises in the Word are for us. *Without faith, it is impossible to please Him, for he who comes to God must believe that He is, and that He Is a rewarder of those who diligently seek Him* (Hebrews 11:6).

Notes and Reflections

Faith to Believe

The following is a word that I received from the Holy Spirit about faith, and I thought I would share it with you:

I created you when I created man in the garden. I put within him my faith. Faith to believe me for the things you think are impossible. Faith should be a natural occurrence for you, no matter what the circumstance is. It is within you. You choose if you will walk by faith or walk in fear. Your mind must be renewed by the Word of God. You must read it every day, meditate on it every day, and purpose in your heart every morning that you are going to walk in faith today.

The enemy wants your mind to be on the natural things in life. Watching television a lot will keep you focused on the things happening in your neighborhood, your city, the state, and the world. As you think about all the things going on in the world, you become fearful, and eventually, you don't trust anyone. You let anger, loneliness, greed, lust, and a lot of other things come in. They bring fear, procrastination, doubt, and unfruitfulness into your life. Instead of meditating on My Word, you were meditating on the things the world has put on your mind. You don't trust Me and My Word. You trust what you see with your natural eyes.

I am a Spirit; you must worship Me in spirit and truth. As you worship me and come into my presence, you will have so much joy and peace. No matter what you see and hear, you will know that I watch over My Word to perform it in your life. I want to do this for you. I want you to have all that I have for you.

Stir up your faith; it is within you. Walk in it; speak it. Every believer has the God kind of faith to speak and see things change. Trust, believe, and obey My voice, My commands, and you will have what you say, as long as you are speaking My Word, not what you feel, but what My Word says about whatever you are going through.

Before you come before Me with a request, make sure your hands are clean, and you have a pure heart. (Who will ascend the hill of the Lord? Those with clean hands and a pure heart (Psalm 24:3-4a)). Ask Me to cleanse you before you approach My throne. Search your heart and ask for forgiveness; repentance is the answer. Expect Me to move; expect Me to meet with you and tell you what to do.

I want you to have the things I have put in your heart. Dream big, see yourself with whatever it is. Faith will cause it to manifest in your life.

Five Practical Steps to Walk by Faith

Following are five practical steps you can follow every day to walk by faith:

1. Study – Read the Word daily (plant the seed, find Scripture to support your request)

2. Let your confessions be in line with the Word (Don't speak negative words about your request.) Confessions will water your seed.

3. Memorize the Scripture you are standing on or write it on an index card and read it several times during the day. Meditate on it (putting fertilizer on your seed.

4. Acknowledge God every day. Thank Him for what He is doing in your life.

5. Praise and worship Him until you see the full manifestation.

Remember a seed does not produce fruit overnight. God has not withheld the fruit just because you do not see it right away. God's timing is not our timing. Continue to water the seed with praise and worship. Praise will still the hand of the enemy. God's got this. Keep praising and keep worshiping until it is manifested. Then continue to thank Him and remind Him of His Word.

Read the following Psalms:

Psalm 103

Psalm 100

Notes and Reflections

Faith for the Journey

As we walk with God, faith will arise in our hearts for the journey. We must be willing to submit our will to His will. Submit yourself to God, and He will give you the desires of your heart (Psalm 37: 4). As we acknowledge Him every day, He will direct our footsteps.

One day, I needed money to pay a bill that I had, so that morning, I asked God for the money when I got up to pray. I pray at 4:00 a.m. Monday through Friday with my friend. We pray for whatever the Holy Spirit directs. After I finished praying with her, I asked for the things that I needed that day. I believed that I was going to receive the money, and I thanked God for it. I got up off my knees from prayer and went into my bedroom, and my husband had put the amount that I needed in my purse. This has happened many times. I expect God to answer my requests, and it comes in different ways. He supplies my needs; because I believe He will answer. My faith in this area has grown from little faith to great faith.

As we petition God for things and believe when we pray, we ask according to His Word. We know we have what we have requested of Him. No matter what the situation is, we can believe God for the answer. There have been many situations in my life where I had to trust God to work things out for me. I might not have received the answer when I thought I needed it, but God did answer. I received it at the right time. We must remember He does not work on our schedule but His own. We only know in part or see a part of the picture. He knows the entire thing, or He sees the whole picture. He knows from the beginning to the end.

God cares about every detail of our lives. When you have an intimate relationship with Him, you share everything with Him. Even though you know He already knows what you are going to say, He wants you to talk to Him about it. *"In all your ways, acknowledge Him, and He will direct your paths."* I ask Him to help me with everything. For example, I ask Him to help me clean my house, and when I do that, I pray as I clean, and before I know it, I have finished. The times that I do not ask Him, it takes me all day to clean my bedroom. So, I have learned to acknowledge Him.

The Holy Spirit is our helper, and He will help us if we ask Him. He helps us to be obedient to the things of God.

The enemy is always busy trying to get us to walk in the flesh. We sometimes yield to the flesh, but we are spirit beings living in a body. We need to walk in the Spirit. The more we acknowledge God, the more we will be led by the Spirit.

I love to shop, but now I am retired and do not need to shop for clothes like I did when I was working. So when I go shopping, I ask the Holy Spirit not to let me buy anything that I do not need. When I see something I really like, I say, "Okay, God. I like this. Can I get it?" Then I go try it on. Most of the time, I yield to the Holy Spirit, and I put it back. If I try the clothes on and they look terrible, I put them back on the rack. If they look good, I have a battle. The flesh wants it, but the Spirit is saying you do not need it. How do you decide to keep it or put it back? I ask myself where are you going to wear this? Do you already have something like this to wear? I know the answer to the questions, so I put it back on the rack and move on. When I have peace, I know I made the right decision.

I do the same thing with eating out. While out riding, I may say to myself, "I want to stop and get something to eat." Immediately the thought comes across my mind, "You have food at home. Save your money." I sometimes laugh at myself because I know the answer, but I will ask anyway. There are plenty of times it is okay to stop and get something. But if I have a bill to pay, why stop to buy something when I have food at home? I know the Holy Spirit is helping me spend my money wisely. *Honor the LORD with your possessions, and with the firstfruits of all your increase; so your barns will be filled with plenty, and your vats will overflow with new wine* (Proverbs 3: 9-10).

Notes and Reflections

Faith to Stand in the Gap
For Your Family

You can ask the Holy Spirit to show you how to stand in the gap for your household's salvation. He is willing and able to show you how to do it. As an intercessor, you must be willing to be a sacrifice for your family. There will be times that you will not be able to do what you want to do because you must spend QUALITY TIME in prayer.

1. Praying the Word over your family

2. Praying in the Spirit (tongues)

3. Fasting

4. Praising and worshipping God

As you begin to pray, things might seem to get worse but continue to pray, and you will eventually see a change. You may get discouraged at times when you are praying, but continue to stand and pray in the Spirit when things seem to be going off track. If you continue to stand, they will get back on track. The enemy does not want to lose those that he has under his control. He will fight to keep them because he knows that once they come into the light of the Word of God, they will beat him on his head. Keep speaking the Word every day over your family. Do not look at what you see with your natural eyes. Keep your eyes on the Word of God. He will honor His Word.

Pray in the Spirit every day for your family, at least an hour or longer, and pray during the day, especially when they come across your mind.

The Scripture the Holy Spirit gave me to stand on for my family is Acts 16:31: *Believe on the Lord Jesus Christ and thou shalt be saved and thy house.* One morning I was praying for my family before I went to work. I had prayed for about an hour, and I decided it was time to get dressed for work. As I went to stand up, the Holy Spirit said, "You don't know what the house is, do you? I said no and, immediately, I saw a church. The church's top came off, and I could see all the people sitting on the pews. The Holy Spirit said, "See all the people on the pews?" I said yes, and He said, "They do not all live in the same house, but this is called the house of the Lord. Then I saw a lot of tents, and He said, "This is the House of Jacob, and they all don't live in one physical tent." There were many tents, but they were called the House of Jacob. Immediately I understood that my family is not just those who lived in my physical house, but all my family members wherever they live. I started praising God because I finally understood that Scripture. I continued to stand on it even today. I know all my family members will be saved. I don't go by what I see or hear with my natural eyes and ears, but by the Word of God. I stood in the gap for approximately two years before I started to see them accept Jesus Christ. I know that before anyone in my family leaves this earth, they will have an opportunity to receive Him as their Lord and Savior. God is faithful, and He watches over His Word to perform it.

When you stand in the gap, you must be persistent and consistent. Every day spend time praying for your family. Every day, confess the Word of God over them. Ask the Holy Spirit to send laborers across their path and for their hearts to be open to receive the Word.

Notes and Reflections

Fear Will Always Try to Come

Fear is an emotion that comes over you when you are asked to do something that you are not comfortable with or asked to do something you do not know how to do. According to the dictionary, fear (noun) is an unpleasant emotion caused by the belief that someone or something is dangerous, likely to cause pain or a threat.

Synonymous words used to convey or describe the unpleasant emotion of fear include terror, fright, fearfulness, horror, alarm, panic, agitation, dread, consternation, dismay, distress, anxiety, worry, unease, uneasiness, apprehension; apprehensiveness, nervousness, nerves, and perturbation. The physical manifestation of fear is listed as foreboding; informally, the creeps, the shivers; the willies, the heebie-jeebies, jitteriness, twitchiness, and butterflies (in the stomach). Extreme, persistent episodes of fear are described as phobias; aversion, antipathy, dread, bugbear, nightmare, horror, terror, anxiety, neurosis, informal hang-ups.

Fear as a verb means to be afraid of (someone or something) as likely to be dangerous, painful, or threatening. Synonyms include be afraid of; be fearful of, be scared of; be apprehensive of; dread; live in fear of, be terrified. Verbs are action words. So, do we choose to surrender calm, control, etc.?

That may seem like a lot of information on fear, but this emotion is so subtle sometimes, and we are always trying to control it. We do not always recognize that we are operating in a spirit of fear. We make decisions sometimes because the underlying motive or reason for the decision is fear.

There are many types of fear, but the Bible says, *"God has not given us a spirit of fear but of power, love, and a sound mind"* (2 Timothy 1:7). Are you making the right decisions based on the Word of God, or are you letting fear play a major role in your decisions?

When we must decide, both faith and fear will come; however, we must decide which road to take. I believe the moment you take a step of faith, fear leaves, but it does not give up. Fear will always try to return, and you will have to say no to that emotion.

Continue to move in faith. Do not say negative things about your decision, do not entertain the thoughts. Cast them down. I cast down negative thoughts by saying out loud, "I am not going to think that way." Sometimes I quote Scripture or sing a praise song, think about something else, or focus on something else. I focus on what God has already done for me—how He gave His life for me so that I might have life and have it more abundantly. I think about how He has delivered so many of my family members out of darkness into His marvelous light and how He healed me when I was sick. I can go on and on about what He had done for me. The Scripture tells us to think on those things that are praiseworthy (Philippians 4: 8). If you have made the right decision, you will have peace and a knowing in your spirit that you have made the right decision, and you will be able to stand.

Our faith grows as we stand on God's Word and when we see the manifestations of the things about which we have prayed. Faith will arise in our hearts if we stand unwavering (Ephesians 4:14 and James 1:6)

Then we will no longer be infants, tossed back and forth by the waves, and blown here and there by every wind of teaching and by the cunning and craftiness of men on their deceitful scheming (Ephesians 4:14 NIV).

But when he asks, he must believe and not doubt because he who doubts is like a wave of the sea, blown and tossed by the wind (James 1:6).

Our creator God has given us what we need to be successful in life. As we go through day to day, our circumstances change, and we change. To be strong, we must face different challenges every day, and the way we handle them helps us grow stronger in faith. Like the process that a caterpillar goes through to become a butterfly, we will go through things that will help us become the person God creates us to be.

Notes and Reflections

Fear Will Keep You in Bondage

According to Dictionary.Com, bondage is (1) Slavery or involuntary servitude, seldom (2) The state of being tied up, chained, or put in handcuffs. From a different perspective, Merriam-Webster defines bondage as (1) the tenure or service of a villain, serf, or slave (2) a state of being bound usually by compulsion (as law or mastery) such as (a) captivity, serfdom (b) servitude or subjugation to a controlling person or force.

For our purpose, it is helpful to understand bondage is a force that can hold you captive. You are not able to do what you would like to do or want to do. You are in a place of standing still and unable to progress or change direction. This causes you to become overwhelmed with fear, and you allow doubt, guilt, and unbelief to overtake you. You do not know which way to go or whose advice to seek. You become bound to the object, person, or circumstance, provoking fear. It is like you are frozen and cannot think or move. You are in bondage at this point.

Fear has put you in bondage. You are being held captive to that thing or situation. Procrastination or hesitancy to take the next step—a corrective action—comes from fear.

We have all types of fear that we do not want to admit we have. We are afraid to even go places outside of our daily or normal routine. We are afraid to make decisions sometimes because we are afraid that we will make the wrong decision. People are afraid to drive on city streets or the beltway, fly, or risk not being good parents. People fear speaking in public, accepting new or different jobs, living alone, or engaging in daily life alone.

The answer to all these fears is JESUS and the Word. Jesus came to set the captives free. He came so that we may have life and have it more abundantly (John 10:10).

When I rededicated my life to Christ and began to study the Word of God, I learned how fear alters the effectiveness of our lives as believers. At a conference I attended, the teacher illustrated how "FEAR" affects the Body of Christ. When hesitant or immobilized in response to fear, we do not do what we were called to do. "FEAR" cripples the sons and daughters of God. At an altar call at the end of the message, he invited everyone dealing with any type of fear to come down front. He was going to break the spirit of fear off us.

I went down front, received prayer, and with others, praised and worshiped God. I believed I was delivered from fear at that moment. While we were advised that the enemy would try to bring the fear back, we were cautioned not to receive it. You are delivered. God has not given you a spirit of fear but power, love, and a sound mind.

The next day I went to work, and my manager asked me to go to a conference in Atlanta, Ga. I agreed immediately. The manager assured me that he would discuss the matter during the next day and make all the arrangements. Although I was excited about going to Atlanta, suddenly, I realized that I would have to fly. I had never flown before. I started to get nervous about flying, and I remembered the conference speaker's word about being free from fear. I said out loud, "I am not afraid to fly. God has set me free."

The next day my manager gave me the information that I needed for the conference. I would pick up my ticket at the American Airlines counter at the airport. My bags were packed. I worked a half-day and traveled to Reagan National Airport. Finding every aspect of my boarding arranged as promised, I waited a few minutes before I was able to board the plane. Excited, I boarded the plane and took my aisle seat. The man across from me spoke to me. I told him this was my first time flying. He smiled and proceeded to tell me everything about the plane, including how they fly in lanes just like cars on highways. He helped me put my seat belt on and adjust my seat. He talked to me the entire flight. Once we landed, he went with me to get my luggage and walked with me outside to get a cab to my hotel. He was so nice and kind to me. He was my angel in disguise. I have never seen him since that time.

I had peace the entire trip. The conference was great. I even had an opportunity to visit my brother in Atlanta before returning home to Washington, D.C. It was a wonderful weekend. God is so good. I have traveled to many places since that time. I love to fly. Today, when I am asked to do something, fear might try to come, but I always remember God has not given me a spirit of fear, and I allow faith and courage to arise in my heart. I move forward. I realize that I can do all things through Christ Jesus. He has not called me to do anything for which He has not already prepared me. He is the one that is doing the work, and I am just a vessel—His servant. I cannot do anything without Him. I am not perfect; I make mistakes sometimes, but I am quick to repent. He continues to help me do the things He has placed in my heart to do.

Notes and Reflections

Notes and Reflections

Testimonials

Faith for the Unexpected

By Patricia A. Jones

As the year 2017 was ending, my life took a turn I never imagined. On the afternoon of November 2, 2017, my oldest daughter, Michelle, passed. My grandson, Andrew, called his wife Melissa to say that his mother had passed suddenly while at work.

Melissa told me. At first, I was unable to comprehend what she was saying. When I understood, it hit me like a ton of bricks. My oldest daughter was gone. I cried until I couldn't cry anymore. We called Monica, my younger daughter, and told her what happened. We all agreed to meet at home and then decided to go where they had taken Michelle. As we got ready to leave for the hospital, my second oldest grandson, Jonathan, arrived home. His reaction was not good at all. Michelle was also his mom.

After we returned from the hospital and I was alone, my thoughts began to get the better of me. I thought only about my loved ones who had passed on: my husband, my mom and dad, my oldest sister, and her oldest son, and now my oldest daughter. Fear and anxiety set in. How many more? My family is so small. I questioned God, but I knew better. I stopped. Thinking back, God had taken care of us and built up my faith to where I could stand again.

Tragedy struck again on the morning of June 18, 2018, when Jonathan passed in his sleep. He had been sick for a while. The sickness manifested itself after his mom passed in 2017.

My heart was broken, and the family was shaken. I had been praying constantly for him and had the prayer group praying for him along with many others. Jonathan was my baby boy even though I had not given birth to him. He and his older brother Andrew had been with me since Jonathan was eight years old.

During all of this, stress set in, and doubt was at the door. We had no way to bury him, but Jesus did. I realized I needed Him so much more now. I couldn't get through all the trauma without Him. I had put Jesus somewhere and was not calling on Him for help, but He was the one source of strength and peace. I have seen God work miracles in my family's lives, which built my faith and encouraged me to hold on to His unchanging love and grace.

Since these experiences, I began to attend the "Grief Share" program offered at Hope Christian Church. This program has helped me to get through and understand some of the various stages of grief I have experienced. I can honestly say I have not completed the journey through grieving. Certain things remind me or trigger thoughts of them. One of the sessions focused on how to respond when friends or family members ask if they can help or do anything for you. I learned just to tell them what I need or let them do what is on their hearts. All of us have or will go through some type of grief at some point in our lives. Rest assured, we all grieve differently, yet the same in some ways. My heart is healing, and that will take time.

I thank my God through Jesus Christ for supplying all our needs according to His riches in glory by Christ Jesus. Whether it is peace, joy, strength, healing, deliverance from fear, or loss of finances, God can and does take care of it. Reach out and call on Him.

How I Overcame Fear of Authority

By Helen Trice

Concerning fear, my perspective is different, as I am sure others have said. I thought about it, prayed, and inquired of God. What came to me was fear is more than just being afraid or scared. Fear for me is rooted in either the truth or a lie. The Word tells me to fear and to fear not. I understand that when He tells me to fear Him, He is not talking about being afraid in the sense of fright—scared and heart racing that stops me in my tracks, and I don't move. He was telling me to honor Him, reverence Him, be ready to adhere to what He says, be in awe and amazement. This fear that is based in truth was the truth of who God is, of His power and might. The truth is that He is a jealous God, God of wrath and compassion and plenteous in mercy.

So, the fear I overcame was of authority. I feared my father, but not in a reverential way. In my eyes, and in my siblings' eyes too, my father ruled not with an iron fist but with an ironing cord. I would ask my mother to ask my father for me for whatever I wanted or thought I needed. I most vividly remember the incident when I was in Junior High School, and Daddy told me not to leave the school grounds during the school day. We lived two blocks from the school. Now I do not remember all the details, nor do I remember how long after he told me that I did just the opposite of what he said. But I remember I left the school grounds one day with three of my friends to go to the store. My father was driving and saw me. Even though I acted like it did not bother me, I saw him knowing I was away from the school grounds. Talking about fear—I was afraid of what he would do, but I knew I was in for a whipping. The very thing I feared happened. I lived through it, and I did not do that again.

In my adult life, working on jobs, I was not one to go crossways of those in authority. B.C. (Before Christ), there were no confrontations or approaches that I remember where I have had to shrink back. I assure you I was not running any sprints to be in any of my bosses' faces. I did procrastinate and put things off as long as I could. I would be stressed, and it was my own doing. A.C. (After Christ) it was the Word in the Book of Job that has encouraged me—knowing all of Job's misfortune was brought on by the enemy and accuser of the brethren. He said, *"What*

I always feared has happened to me. What I dreaded has come true" (Job.3:25 NLT). For me, it may not be as simple as I am saying; I am not to be fearful like that. Job feared it, and it happened. It helped me to understand I can bring things on myself. It has given me somewhat of boldness, not arrogance. I am not saying that fear does not try to come when I must deal with certain people in authority, but I pray, asking for wisdom and guidance about what I should say or do.

One time I made an error (I have made more than one), and I did not want to tell my boss. Fear of authority rose in me; my thoughts were, "I will tell her; I will resign," before I had even approached her. I was praying, but when there is anxiety, I cannot hear from God. It was not like I had a whole lot of time. Anyway, after trying to justify the error and pray, I humbled myself and let my boss know what I had done. The error was resolved, and I did not have to resign, nor was I let go.

I am reminded of Jeremiah 1:8 (NLT): *And don't be afraid of the people, for I will be with you and will protect you. I, the LORD, have spoken!* For me, this says, "Fear not authority."

How I Overcame My Issue with Fear

By Myra Thomas

I was not particularly adventurous as a child, , but I was curious about things and how they worked. On one occasion, I challenged myself to ride a roller-coaster. Later, as an adult, I developed an interest in swimming, so I decided to take classes at a local YMCA near work. A clumsy swimmer, somehow, I did learn to float and tread water. I remained uncomfortable with swimming; I think it was mostly about not being able to touch the bottom of the pool and being fearful that I could drown. On my final day of swimming class, I had to dive into the deep end and float to the top to pass the class. I was terrified even though I had a safety net—the instructor was going to be in the pool with me.

My most challenging bout with fear happened in 2011. One day while driving across a bridge, I had a panic attack, and anxiety took control. I was scared beyond anything I can explain. For months I could not look at a bridge or overpass or even think about sitting in the upper section at a stadium. I avoided all things where I had to deal with height. I would drive longer routes to most of my destinations to avoid highways with the least amount of elevation to them. At one point, travel in bumper-to-bumper, rush hour traffic was my haven. I felt safe when I was surrounded by other cars and trucks. I soon realized that I could not live this way. I did not have the luxury or means to have a driver. I needed my freedom back, so I sought the help of a therapist.

We made great progress. I remember so vividly the day I looked at a tall bridge, and my heart did not race as if it was going to jump out of my chest. I could barely wait to call my therapist to give her the good news. I looked and felt nothing. It was liberating, but I was still afraid to drive on a bridge. I made several attempts but just couldn't bring myself to do it. I was doing the right things from a clinical perspective, but I needed more. Prayer would be the answer.

One Sunday during altar call, I decided to give it to the Lord. Why am I trying to deal with this thing in my strength? I went up and laid fear and anxiety on the altar. For months, I prayed and sought favor to be delivered from this stronghold. I knew that the Lord was my light and my salvation. I did not have to fear anything or anyone. Psalm 27:1 is one of my favorite Scriptures: *The Lord is my light and my salvation; whom shall I fear?* Deuteronomy 31:6 lets me know when I am doubtful and weak, God is with me always. He will never leave me. It reads, *"Be strong and courageous. Do not be afraid or terrified because of them, for the Lord your God goes with you; He will never leave you nor forsake you."*

Psalm 118:6-7 reaffirms that I am never alone: *The Lord is with me; I will not be afraid. What can man do to me? The Lord is with me; He is my helper.* Proverbs 28:25 says, *"Fear of man will prove to be a snare, but whoever trusts in the Lord is kept safe."* These Scriptures have been my lifesaver; God's Word is powerful. Today, I continue to see myself as an overcomer, yet I know there is still work to be done. Whenever I feel a level of anxiety bubbling up inside, I'm confident in knowing that God's promises still stand. I can do all things through Christ Jesus who strengthens me.

Casting Out Fear
By Receiving God's Love

By Donna Mazyck

As we traveled down the road, I looked in the rearview mirror at my seven-year-old son and asked, "How are you doing with feelings of fear?" My son replied, "I am doing better now that I see you doing better." Throughout my childhood and into the decades of my 20s and 30s, fear occupied a prominent place in my thoughts and feelings. I tried memorizing and meditating on Scriptures that spoke of overcoming fear. I resolved to increase my faith in order to decrease fear of rejection, fear of failure, and fear of displeasing people.

When I noticed my young son's fear of being hospitalized, it reflected fears that I lived with daily. So, I set out to share with him ways of conquering fear and, at times, moving forward despite the fear. I had not told him my struggles with fear, but he saw them. It was time for me to confront myself and get to the root of the fears on which I functioned.

My awareness of a root cause of fear in my life first emerged when I learned that my 10-day old son was diagnosed with a chronic health disease. It was caused by a genetic condition resulting from recessive traits carried by my husband and me. I remember wondering what I had done wrong for my son to be diagnosed with this disease. Logically, I pushed back on the notion that my punishment for doing or being wrong was having my child suffer from a chronic health problem. Emotionally, I was saddened by the thought that it was my fault. I spent days and nights fearing the worse.

As I prayed about fear, listened to teachings about fear, and read Scriptures about fear, I began to understand that faith alone would not conquer fear. A one size fits all formula does not generally decrease fear in our lives. What diminished root issues of fear in my life was love—believing, receiving, and speaking about love that would not let me go—Love, who is the Lord God Almighty. The truth resided in the Bible verses I had read and memorized over the years. I learned to receive, believe, and speak the truth. This life-changing process occurred over the years. I saw life circumstances with different lenses. My prayers began to reflect the reality of my position: I am loved unconditionally and deeply.

Scriptures that helped me make the exchange from fear to love include:

Faith vs. Fear

For God will never give you the spirit of fear, but the Holy Spirit who gives you mighty power, love, and self-control (2 Timothy 1:7 TPT).

Love never brings fear, for fear is always related to punishment. But love's perfection drives the fear of punishment far from our hearts. Whoever walks constantly afraid of punishment has not reached love's perfection (1 John 4:18 TPT).

But in the day that I'm afraid, I lay all my fears before You and trust in You with all my heart (Psalm 56:3 TPT).

Listen to my testimony: I cried to God in my distress, and He answered me. He freed me from all my fears (Psalm 34:4 TPT).

Lord, even when Your path takes me through the valley of deepest darkness, fear will never conquer me, for You already have! You remain close to me and lead me through it all the way. Your authority is my strength and my peace. The comfort of Your love takes away my fear. I'll never be lonely, for You are near (Psalm 23:4 TPT).

54

Now I know, Lord, that you are for me, and I will never fear what man can do to me (Psalm 118:6 TPT).

So, what does all this mean? If God has determined to stand with us, tell me, who then could ever stand against us? (Romans 8:31 TPT).

In addition to reading, meditating on, and memorizing Scriptures, I began another habit that helped me open up to God's love for me. Give thanks. Gratitude for the gifts in my life, e.g., health, sunshine, provision, and more opened me to the Giver of all good gifts, the Lord. The chorus of a hymn I sang in church services as a little girl described the transformation I experienced: *Love lifted me; love lifted me. When nothing else could help, love lifted me.* The perfect love of God cast out my fears.

About the Author

Brenda Williams exemplifies the love of Christ in every aspect of her life. She is a mentor, an encourager, and more importantly, a woman of faith and prayer. She has a passion to see women healed, delivered, and set free so that they can fulfill the destiny God has ordained for them.

In September 2005, Brenda was ordained an Associate Pastor at Hope Christian Church under the leadership of Bishop Harry R. Jackson, Jr., and serves in several ministries. She has been a teacher in the Delta Force Bible College Program and served as head of the Usher Ministry and Women's Ministry for several years. Brenda, along with several other women, founded Women in Fellowship over 25 years ago and she has been faithfully serving as the President since its conception. She is the author of *"A Walk with the Father: Intimate Relationship."*

For those who know her well, it is not the titles nor the number of ministries she serves in that makes her the great woman that she is, it is the heart that she has to see people, especially women, whole. Brenda's lifestyle is best summed up in her favorite passage of Scripture, Psalm 34.

Brenda worked in the banking industry for over 35 years and is retired from the Library of Congress Federal Credit Union. Her devotion and commitment to Christ can be seen as she continues to be a demonstration of the love of God.

Brenda has been happily married for 52 years to Willie Williams, and they have two children, one grandchild, and one great-grandchild.

A WALK WITH THE FATHER

INTIMATE RELATIONSHIP

BRENDA WILLIAMS

(ISBN: 978-0-9799798-2-8)

Available wherever books are sold.

Contact

To inquire about the author doing book signings, speaking, or ministering at your event, please contact her at

bowilliams1969@gmail.com

For information on ordering copies of *Faith vs. Fear*, please contact the author or Kingdom Living Publishing:

Kingdom Living Publishing

P.O. Box 660

Accokeek, Maryland 20607

publish@kingdomlivingbooks.com

(301) 275-9014